P9-APP-000

CHOLERA

CHOLERA

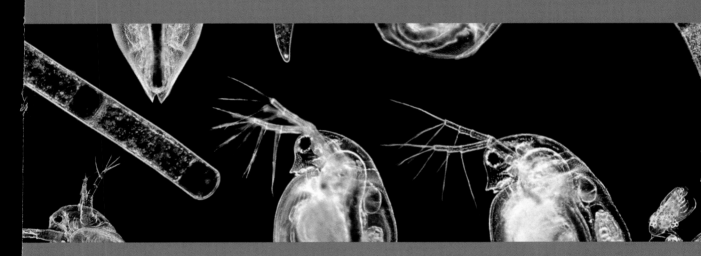

Ruth Bjorklund

Marshall Cavendish
Benchmark
New York

Special thanks to Dr. Richard L. Guerrant, director of the Center for Global Health at the University of Virginia School of Medicine, for his expert review of the manuscript.

Other Marshall Cavendish Offices:
Marshall Cavendish International (Asia) Private Limited, 1 New Industrial Road, Singapore 536196 • Marshall Cavendish International (Thailand) Co Ltd. 253 Asoke, 12th Flr, Sukhumvit 21 Road, Klongtoey Nua, Wattana, Bangkok 10110, Thailand • Marshall Cavendish (Malaysia) Sdn Bhd, Times Subang, Lot 46, Subang Hi-Tech Industrial Park, Batu Tiga, 40000 Shah Alam, Selangor Darul Ehsan, Malaysia

Marshall Cavendish is a trademark of Times Publishing Limited

All websites were available and accurate when this book was sent to press.

Library of Congress Cataloging-in-Publication Data

Bjorklund, Ruth.
Cholera / by Ruth Bjorklund.
p. cm. — (Health alert)
Summary: "Provides comprehensive information on the causes, treatment, and history of cholera"—Provided by publisher.
Includes index.
ISBN 978-0-7614-4820-4
1. Cholera—Juvenile literature. I. Title.
RC126.B56 2011
616.9'32—dc22
2009051253

Front Cover: A close-up look at Vibrio Cholerae, the bacteria that causes Cholera.
Title page: A close-up look at water fleas, which carry the Cholera bacteria.

Photo Research by Candlepants Incorporated
Cover Photo: 3D4Medical.com/Getty Images

The photographs in this book are used by permission and through the courtesy of:
Getty Images: Laguna Design, 3; George Grall, 12; 14, 31, 35, 42; Farjana K. Godhuly/AFP, 18, 41; Justin Sullivan, 22; Dario Mitidieri, 25; Wissam Al-Okaili/AFP, 52. *Alamy Images*: medicalpicture, 5, 11; Jenny Matthews, 21; Phototake Inc., 37; Streetfly Stock, 47; Irene Abdou, 48; qaphotos.com, 50. *AP Images*: Tsvangirayi Mukwazhi, 8, 17, 55. *The Image Works*: TopFoto, 33.

Editor: Joy Bean
Publisher: Michelle Bisson
Art Director: Anahid Hamparian

Printed in Malaysia (T)
6 5 4 3 2 1

CONTENTS

1

A STORY OF CHOLERA

On nearly every continent, some people do not have access to clean water or **sewage** disposal systems. In places such as this, cholera claims more than 100,000 lives each year. While not all people who are diagnosed with cholera die, international health organizations say that cholera affects millions of people every year.

"People see it as a dirty disease," says a cholera expert with the World Health Organization (WHO). "People don't want to talk about it." Government officials don't want to talk about cholera either, she adds. Governments of many poor or undeveloped countries report only a fraction of cholera cases to the United Nations or WHO each year. Government leaders fear that if people view their country as dirty, tourists won't visit and companies will not want to do business there. Because so many cases of cholera go unreported, too many people have become infected or dangerously ill. And too many people have died.

A nurse with the international health organization Doctors Without Borders described the struggles of one family in Zimbabwe, Africa. Here is their story.

The nurse was working in a small community health clinic. One night she received a call from another nurse. The nurse on night duty had been told that a mother and her children, who appeared very sick, were seen stopped along a road. The nurses had a curfew, so they were not allowed to travel outside their medical compound at night. But at sunrise, two clinic nurses packed up some medicine and emergency first aid supplies and drove toward the distant villages. They hoped to find the family, but they were also frightened about what they might see.

After two hours of searching, the nurses found the mother and her six children in their village. They were all extremely weak. Their bodies were skin and bones, and they could barely move or breathe. The father had already died.

The nurses knew that the family's only chance of survival was to get them to the clinic as quickly as possible. In the meantime, the nurses gave them much-needed **intravenous (IV)** fluids and nutrients. IV fluids get into the body quickly because they are inserted through a hollow needle into a patient's vein.

There was little time to delay. The nurses felt that if they had found the family any later, their lives would be lost, yet

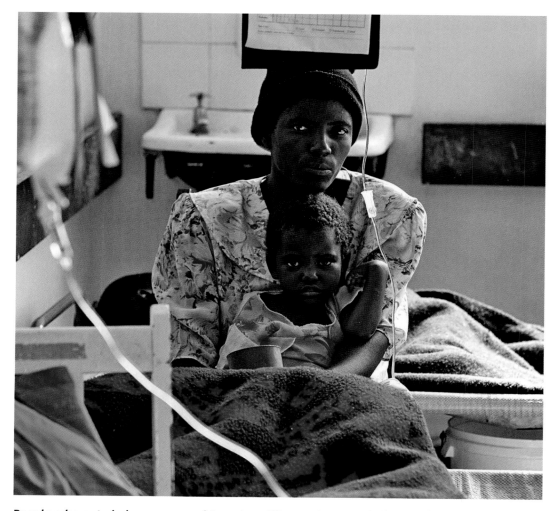

People who get cholera may need to get an IV to make sure their bodies do not lose too many fluids.

they were still very much in danger. The nurses' car was small, so they had to pack the family in tightly. Some members even had to lie on top of one other. As the car banged along the rough roads, the nurses did all they could to comfort the children and their mother. None of them could speak, and most had trouble breathing. Some writhed in pain from muscle cramps, while others vomited. All of them quietly groaned in agony.

After several days of receiving medicine, fluids, and essential nutrients called **electrolytes**, the mother and her children began to recover. The mother told the nurses that a few days earlier, her husband had gone to the funeral of someone who had died of cholera. Soon afterward, her husband had fallen ill. After suffering greatly from **diarrhea** and vomiting, he had died. On the day her husband passed away, she and her children had begun to vomit and to suffer from diarrhea. She knew that they were going to get sick, but she had no money or means of getting to the nearest clinic 30 miles (50 kilometers) away. Her neighbors were afraid of catching the disease and refused to help the family. The mother started walking toward the clinic, but she and her family were too weak to get very far, so they returned to their home in the village. The mother gave up all hope, and she was in utter disbelief when the nurses found them and cured them.

This family was luckier than most people who live without clean water, toilets, proper sewage treatment, and basic medical care. Cholera is rarely a threat in a developed country such as the United States, but it unnecessarily destroys the lives of people in impoverished regions throughout the world.

2

WHAT IS CHOLERA?

Cholera is a water-borne, and sometimes food-borne, disease. It is easily diagnosed, easily treated, and curable—if it is caught in time. Cholera is spread through **contamination** of drinking water or food, poor hygiene, and unsanitary conditions. Caused by the tiny **bacterium *Vibrio cholerae***, cholera multiplies quickly in the body's intestines and can make a victim sick within a few hours.

When a person eats or drinks something infected with *Vibrio cholerae*, the bacteria reproduce rapidly in the body's intestines. The bacteria are not the actual culprit in producing the disease. Rather, cholera bacteria create a powerful poison called **cholera toxin (CTX)**. The CTX attaches to the walls of the intestines and interrupts the flow of electrolytes in and out

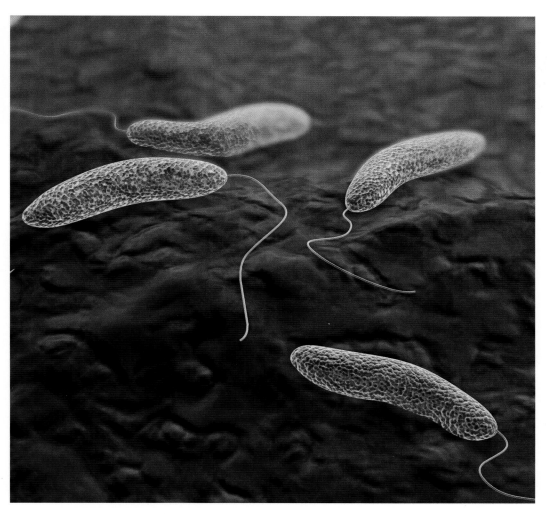

A close-up look at the bacteria that causes cholera.

of the body's tissues. The body reacts by draining itself of huge amounts of water. Electrolytes and water stop circulating to the brain, kidneys, and other organs. People often faint, and they may die in just a few hours.

HOW IS CHOLERA TRANSMITTED?

In their natural environment, cholera bacteria live in tiny sea creatures called **copepods.** Thousands of bacteria can exist on a single copepod. The copepods travel throughout the oceans of the world in search of food—plankton and algae—that is found in higher concentrations in coastal areas. In spring and in fall, ocean temperatures along shorelines rise and cause

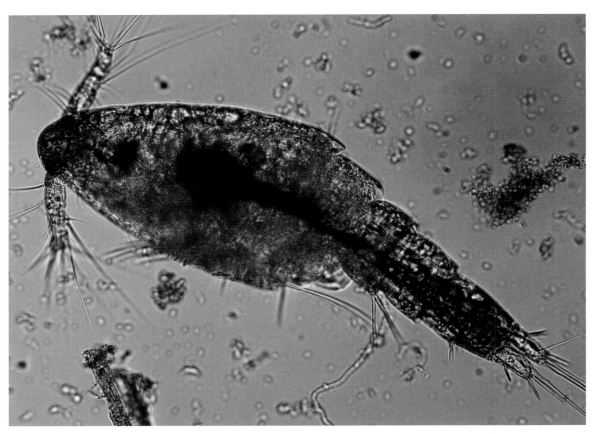

This copepod is magnified ninety times. It uses its antennae to move itself in the water.

major increases in plankton and algae. Large populations of plankton and algae mean large populations of infected copepods.

Shorelines also become contaminated when human waste drains into the water, or when manure and fertilizers from farms are flushed into the sea. This type of pollution causes the algae to multiply even more. With the increase in food supply, copepods gather and rapidly reproduce, and as the creatures reproduce, so do the cholera bacteria.

When people eat raw fish and seafood that is contaminated with cholera bacteria, they do not become sick instantly. But the bacteria multiply, produce CTX, and often cause cholera diarrhea in one to two days. In other people, the bacteria live in their intestines for up to two weeks or longer and are shed from their bodies in their **feces**. In areas with poor waste treatment, the cholera bacteria in the feces enter the food and water supplies. Improper processing or disposal of human sewage causes the bacteria to filter down through the soil and enter the groundwater.

Then the bacteria spread to more people as they drink dirty water from shared wells. Farmers pollute their crops when they use the dirty water to irrigate their fields. Farmers can also contaminate crops when they spread untreated manure from infected animals or humans on their soil. As people eat the food, the cycle continues and the cholera infestation increases.

A boy crosses over an open ditch of dirty, untreated water, a breeding ground for cholera bacteria.

The more cholera bacteria people ingest, the greater the likelihood that they will get the disease. It takes about a million cholera bacteria to cause sickness. That may sound like a lot, but that amount can exist in a single glass of water that does not even look dirty.

SYMPTOMS

Most people who become infected with cholera receive treatment or experience only mild **symptoms**, so they do not become seriously ill. However, 5 to 10 percent of people develop a more severe infection. The people who are most likely to get sick are the young, the old, the undernourished, and the weak. Also at risk are people with type O blood, people with insufficient stomach acids, and also people with weak immune systems. According to WHO, untreated cholera in its most potent form can kill a healthy adult in a matter of hours.

The main symptom of cholera is sudden, watery diarrhea. In a milder bacterial infection, diarrhea is actually a helpful response. In normal digestion, food moves through the intestines slowly so that fluids and nutrients can be absorbed into the bloodstream. But when the body becomes infected with bacteria, the mucus lining of the intestines becomes irritated and inflamed. In order to flush away the harmful bacteria, the muscles around the intestines squeeze the intestines and push the food and bacteria out of the body quickly.

Zimbabwe's Outbreak

Beginning in August 2008, the country of Zimbabwe has suffered the worst cholera **epidemic** in more than fifteen years. The disease has infiltrated each of the ten provinces that make up the country. More than 100,000 people have come down with the disease, and more than 4,000 people have died.

Zimbabwe is an underdeveloped African country with very poor **water purification** and sanitation systems. Aid groups from around the world have been in Zimbabwe since December 2008 to try and combat the massive **outbreak**. Even though the disease can be treated and cured relatively quickly, the real problem lies in the cause of the outbreaks. The country desperately needs clean water, toilets, and proper sewage treatment. The International Red Cross and similar relief organizations are trying to help by drilling new wells, improving the quality of pipes that carry water, and teaching villagers about hygiene. The Red Cross has stated that in a year's time, they have given more than a half million people access to clean water. Zimbabwean government officials have announced that it will take many years before they can build and improve their water supply and sanitation systems.

Children in Zimbabwe collect stagnant water for use in their home. Using water that has not been purified can lead to cholera.

Young children are at high risk for getting cholera because their bodies do not have a strong immune system like healthy adults do.

Cholera diarrhea is not a healthy response, however. It is formed from a combination of mucus, dead cells, and quarts of extra water and electrolytes. The diarrhea is milky in color and has small particles that look like bits of rice. **Dehydration** due to cholera diarrhea is especially dangerous because the body loses so much fluid—nearly a quart per hour—in a very short period of time.

As the disease unfolds, it can lead to other symptoms such as vomiting, muscle cramps, dehydration, kidney failure, and shock. Children may suffer from low blood sugar. The main source of the body's energy is sugar, which comes from food. Cholera prevents people from being able to digest their food properly, so the levels of sugar in their blood drop dramatically. This condition is called **hypoglycemia**. Hypoglycemia leads to seizures or a loss of consciousness, especially in children. Vomiting occurs when the lining of the stomach becomes irritated. Messages from nerves trigger the brain's vomit center, which causes the stomach muscles to contract and to force the contents of the stomach up and out of the body through the mouth. A person with a severe case of cholera may vomit for hours at a time, especially at the onset of the disease. Once the stomach is completely emptied, vomiting tends to stop, but the victim will experience painful abdominal cramps because the stomach muscles will continue to contract.

Frequent vomiting and diarrhea result in severe loss of essential minerals such as sodium, chloride, and potassium. This causes leg muscles to cramp and interferes with normal movement. Soon after a cholera infection worsens, the victim experiences dehydration symptoms such as loss of body weight, exhaustion, sunken eyes, extreme thirst, and dry, wrinkled skin. The disease also affects blood pressure. When blood pressure sinks too low, the blood cannot transport enough oxygen to nourish the cells of the body. In extreme cases, this causes **hypovolemic shock**, which can quickly lead to death.

Vibrio cholerae is one of the most common disease-causing bacteria on Earth. Worldwide, an estimated 200,000 to 1 million cases occur every year. Cholera has a huge impact on developing areas in places such as India, Asia, Russia, the Middle East, Central and South America, and sub-Saharan Africa. Regions become particularly vulnerable when they have suffered from war or natural disasters such as floods, hurricanes, tsunamis, or earthquakes. These catastrophes uproot people from their homes and communities. Many must seek aid in crowded refugee camps. These camps are located on unused land that is generally unused for a reason: it lacks adequate water or **sanitary** facilities. When people live very close together and lack food, clean water, and basic medical care, cholera spreads quickly.

Developed countries with modern sewage and water treatment systems rarely report cases of cholera. In the United States, there are generally fewer than five reported cases of cholera per year. Occasionally cholera contaminates shellfish in port areas, where ocean going ships have brought in copepods carrying cholera bacteria. Travelers carrying the

Rwandan refugees live at a refugee camp in 1994. Close quarters and lack of sanitary facilities can create an environment in which cholera can be spread easily.

In some port areas, an outbreak of Cholera can occur when people eat contaminated shellfish.

disease from other places can also introduce cholera to otherwise cholera-free areas. International health organizations are trying to supply impoverished areas with life-saving medical care and information about prevention, good hygiene, and sanitation. More important, health workers promote a global effort to help the governments of underdeveloped countries create water treatment systems that would eliminate the causes of cholera altogether.

3

THE HISTORY OF CHOLERA

Cholera has probably caused illness for centuries, but the first time an outbreak came to light was in 1817 in Kolkata, India (once known as Calcutta). From India, the disease spread to Southeast Asia, central Asia, the Middle East, and Russia. By 1824, cholera had sickened countless people and had killed hundreds of thousands.

The source of the outbreak was the Ganges River, which is considered the lifeblood of India. The Ganges flows the length of the country and supplies its people with water for drinking, washing, irrigation, and waste removal. Scientists think that cholera was **endemic** to the Ganges River and that low levels of the bacteria had been present as far back as 400 B.C.E. An endemic disease exists only in a certain region. But in 1817, cholera would become more than a regional problem.

Since 1817, millions of people travel to the Ganges River in India to celebrate the Kumbh Mela festival. An unsanitary environment is created when the people bathe in and drink from the river.

Timeline of Known
Cholera Pandemics

. . . .

First Pandemic: 1817–1823

The disease started in the Ganges River region and spread to Kolkata, India. Then soldiers and traders carried it to Southeast Asia, central Asia, the Middle East, eastern Africa, and the Mediterranean.

Second Pandemic: 1829–1849

It began in India and was taken by traders and merchants to Russia, Finland, Poland, and, in 1831, England. Irish immigrants carried the disease to Quebec, Canada, in 1832, and then it entered the United States through Detroit, Michigan, and New York. By 1832, cholera had reached New Orleans, and by 1833 it had journeyed to Mexico.

Third Pandemic: 1852–1859

From India, British troops carried cholera to Afghanistan, and then it moved into China, Iran, Asia, Africa, and Europe. Europeans carried the bacteria to the east coast of the United States. In 1849, California gold rush miners carried the disease from the east coast to the Pacific coast and Mexico. *Vibrio cholerae* reached Central America in 1856.

Fourth Pandemic: 1863–1879
As they traveled to their holy land, Muslim pilgrims took cholera from the Ganges Delta to Mecca, Saudi Arabia. From there the disease spread to the Middle East, Africa, western Europe, Russia, and the Americas.

Fifth Pandemic: 1881–1896
During this pandemic, *Vibrio cholerae* spread from the Kolkata region of India to Asia, Africa, South America, France, Russia, Germany, and Japan.

Sixth Pandemic: 1899–1823
Once again, the outbreak started in the Ganges River region. Then it reached the Middle East, North Africa, and Russia.

Seventh Pandemic: 1961–Present
Originating in Indonesia, the cholera bacteria known as *El Tor* spread across Asia, reached Europe, and then hit the Middle East and Africa. In 1991, it reappeared in Peru.

Kumbh Mela is an important Hindu festival celebrated every twelve years. In 1817, millions of people attended Kumbh Mela in a city along the Upper Ganges River. For three months, the people drank from, washed in, and defecated in the river. Many became sick at the site, while others unknowingly carried the cholera bacteria home with them and infected their community water supplies. In cities across India, people became sick and died from vomiting, diarrhea, and dehydration.

In the crowded city of Kolkata, the disease became an epidemic. A disease is epidemic when it spreads rapidly from community to community. But Kolkata was also a port city and a major trade center. Before long, foreign traders, businesspeople, sailors, and soldiers carried the cholera bacteria back to their distant homes. Cholera became a pandemic, or worldwide, disease. The pandemic did not end until 1824. Scientists think that the spread of cholera came to a halt because of an extremely cold winter. Two years later, however, cholera reared up again. Like the first pandemic, it spread to Asia, the Middle East, and Russia, but it also hit Western Europe. From Europe, people carried cholera across the Atlantic Ocean to North America.

Since that time, there have been five more cholera pandemics. A new **strain** of the cholera bacteria was discovered in Bangladesh in 1992. Many of the medicines used to combat the old strain may not be as useful with the new bacteria.

In recent decades, there have been several cholera epidemics in areas around the world, such as Peru, Indonesia, Bangladesh, and the African countries of Mozambique, Democratic Republic of the Congo, Tanzania, Rwanda, and Zimbabwe. Scientists fear that with fewer medicines to fight the new bacteria strain, the world could see an eighth cholera pandemic soon.

NINETEENTH-CENTURY MEDICAL RESEARCH

During the second and third pandemics, doctors in England began to investigate the causes of cholera and other infectious diseases. Many people believed that diseases were punishments or warnings from God. That theory gave way to the idea that infectious diseases such as cholera were transmitted through **miasma**, or "bad air." Nineteenth-century cities were over-crowded, and poor neighborhoods were foul smelling and filled with trash. There were no sewage systems, and waste often filled the streets. Public water supplies were mostly unsafe to drink. With minimal access to clean water, sanitary living conditions, and good health care, poor people were much more likely to suffer from disease and other health problems than the wealthier classes. Medical professionals thus concluded that the foul-smelling air caused by human waste and garbage was what spread so much disease among poor city dwellers and low-wage workers.

In 1842, an English politician named Edwin Chadwick

studied patterns of disease outbreaks, particularly among low-wage workers. He submitted to the British Parliament a report called *The Sanitary Conditions of the Labouring Population of Great Britain*. The report included a study by two British doctors called "Physical Causes of Fever in the Metropolis, which might be Removed by Proper Sanitary Measures." Chadwick's report was the first to introduce the idea that a lack of sanitation in poor neighborhoods could cause disease.

Chadwick also was very concerned about the cycle of poverty and ill health that kept poor people poor. In other words, when low-wage workers became sick, they lost their jobs and their families were cast into deeper poverty. Poverty, he believed, was the root of overcrowding and unsanitary living conditions. Chadwick urged the government to enact laws that would provide clean water and waste removal for poor neighborhoods. In 1848, the British Parliament passed the Public Health Act, establishing water purification and sewage and trash disposal projects.

Another London government official, William Farr, studied the locations of one cholera outbreak. He noticed that the people living closest to the Thames River were more likely to develop cholera than people away from the river, where there was good sewage disposal. Still, Farr believed that the foul-smelling air, rather than the water coming from the Thames River, had caused the cholera outbreak.

Edwin Chadwick was an English economist and social reformer who helped create an awareness for the causes of cholera.

In 1831, John Snow, an eighteen-year-old medical student, was called to a small English village called Newcastle-Upon-Tyne. He was asked to help local mine workers who had become terribly ill. Snow instantly recognized that the miners suffered from cholera. Although he was young, Snow was familiar with the disease because so many people in England had brought the disease back with them from India.

Deeply affected by the miners' suffering, after Snow graduated from medical school in 1844, he continued to study contagious diseases. When cholera broke out in London in 1848, Snow made maps showing concentrations of cholera cases. His maps showed clusters of cases in the vicinities of particular water supplies. This evidence convinced him that the disease was spread by water and not by miasmas.

Snow noticed a curious pattern in a village called Horsleydown. On one side of a street was a row of cottages called Truscott's Court, and on the other side of the street was a row of cottages called the Surrey Buildings. Both neighborhoods dumped their sewage into the same canal. However, many of the people living in the Surrey Buildings came down with cholera, while those living in Truscott's Court did not. It turned out that the sewage leaked into the drinking well belonging to the Surrey Buildings, but it did not leak into the well at Truscott's Court. This further linked dirty water to cholera.

John Snow helped identify patterns in cholera epidemics.

Advances in Fighting Disease

Robert Koch was a brilliant researcher in the field of the "germ theory" of disease. He was one of a few forward thinkers who did not believe that diseases floated around in puffs of bad air. He believed that **microorganisms**, or germs, were at the root of disease. In his laboratory, Koch set out to isolate disease-causing germs from harmless organisms. In order to accomplish this task, he had to separate the germs from other microorganisms and grow them into germ colonies large enough to study. Using his methods, known as the Koch postulates, he discovered the germs that cause tuberculosis, diphtheria, anthrax, dysentery, and other diseases.

Unlike other researchers who used laboratory flasks, Koch grew his specimens in a thick broth, or gelatin, on glass plates. He said this method prevented contamination. But while he was researching cholera, he had difficulty getting the bacteria to grow because the gelatin turned to a liquid at the higher temperatures needed for *Vibrio cholerae* to multiply. F. E. Hesse, the wife of one of Koch's research assistants, solved this problem. She had learned of an Indonesian jelly-making technique that used a type of seaweed called agar-agar. Hesse suggested that her husband try agar as a growth medium for the cholera bacteria. It worked—so well, in fact, that scientists still use it in laboratories today.

An assistant named Julius Richard Petri also influenced Koch's laboratory procedures. Normally, Koch used glass plates to hold his specimens, but the plates required careful handling. Petri designed a glass dish with a lid that allowed easy access to the bacteria while also keeping the specimens sterile. Today, Petri dishes are a staple of laboratories around the world.

Robert Koch won the 1905 Nobel Prize in Physiology or Medicine.

In 1854, while another cholera epidemic ravaged London, Snow mapped the various cases and saw that the highest concentrations occurred in neighborhoods near the Broad Street public water pump. Snow could not yet prove that water from the Broad Street pump had caused the infection, because some cholera victims did not live near the pump. Snow visited the family of a woman living in a suburb of London. The woman had died of cholera, but none of her family members or neighbors were sick. After questioning servants and relatives, Snow discovered that the woman had preferred the water from the Broad Street pump and had sent a servant to fetch her some. She drank it, fell ill shortly afterward, and died.

With this information, Snow felt he had honed in on the source of the cholera epidemic. But he still had one or two more mysteries to solve. For example, there was a brewery close to the Broad Street pump, but the factory workers there did not become ill. It turned out that the owner of the brewery encouraged his workers to drink beer instead of water. Thus he unknowingly saved his employees from a terrible fate. Snow felt this confirmed his theory, and he asked the city to remove the handle on the Broad Street pump. When authorities investigated, they discovered that a nearby sewer pipe had leaked into the Broad Street well. Today, Snow is considered the father of modern **epidemiology**, which is the science of studying patterns and occurrences of diseases among groups of people.

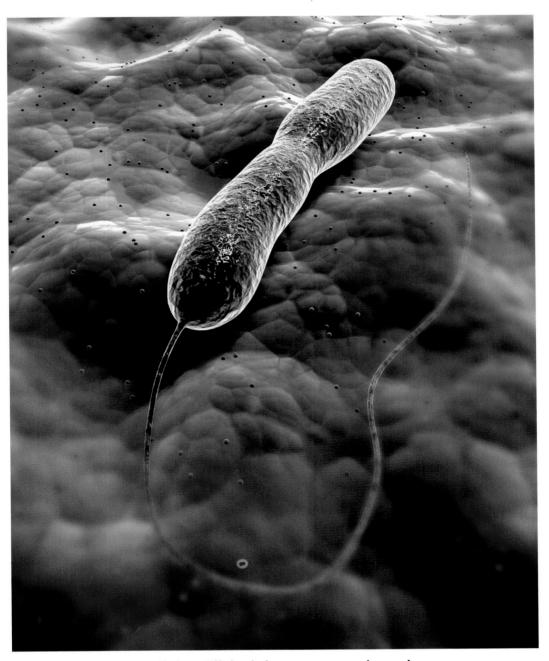

The bacteria that causes Cholera, Vibrio cholerae, as seen under a microscope.

In the same year that John Snow demonstrated how cholera was spread, an Italian doctor named Filippo Pacini discovered the bacterium *Vibrio cholerae*. Other Italian doctors ignored his achievement, however, because they still believed that miasma caused the disease. Not until 1883 did another doctor, a German physician named Robert Koch, rediscover the bacterium independently of Pacini's discovery. This time, medical experts paid attention. Doctors in western Europe and North America had finally accepted the idea that disease was not caused by bad air but by microorganisms, such as viruses and bacteria.

DEFEATING CHOLERA

In 1849, a New York doctor named C. B. Coventry wrote a reference book about treating cholera. He described the disease in four stages: "premonitory" (the start-up phase), "cramps, diarrhea, and coldness," "collapse," and "consecutive fever." Coventry had a plan for each stage. For the first stage, the doctor prescribed bed rest and tea. If the patient had eaten, he suggested that he or she take medicine to induce vomiting. He also believed the patient should be bled—"The object of the bleeding is to relieve the internal congestion," he wrote—but the bleeding should be discontinued if the victim fainted.

At the second stage, Coventry advised doctors to put the patient's feet and legs in warm water with mustard and salt, then to "open a vein in the arm, and bleed from five to sixteen to twenty ounces." He also suggested giving the patient powerful medicines such as calomel, opium, camphor, and sulfuric ether. Each of these "cures" had devastating side effects. Coventry also recommended chicken tea and salt at this stage.

For the third stage, Coventry called for more calomel, camphor, and bloodletting. By this time, however, the patient had little chance of survival. If the victim made it to the fourth stage, Dr. Coventry prescribed more calomel, opium, and leeches (to suck the blood), as well as morphine and magnesia.

Doctors in Europe and North America debated the merits of various cures. Many doctors were against prescribing castor oil or other medicines that induce vomiting or diarrhea. Some found success with bed rest plus tea or drops of strong coffee. A New York physician, W. Rhinelander, suggested that patients should be given a saline (salt) solution directly into their veins. Modern-day doctors recognize that Rhinelander was on the right track.

In the 1860s, health officials in the United States were convinced that because they knew the causes of cholera, they had it under control. Big cities such as Chicago and New York began major public sanitation projects. Health departments spread the word about improving health habits such as hand washing, using toilets, cleaning raw vegetables thoroughly, cooking foods to safe temperatures, and avoiding or boiling any water that might be contaminated. Still, outbreaks occurred. So, in addition to educating people and protecting the water supply, health care professionals had to develop efficient and successful ways of treating cholera victims.

By the end of the nineteenth century, doctors recognized that replacing a cholera patient's body fluids was key to survival. They treated their most dehydrated patients with IV saline solutions that contained the electrolytes that the body needs to maintain a normal fluid balance. Once the patients got better, doctors encouraged them to eat healthy foods to strengthen their weakened bodies.

Today, cholera treatment resembles the successful treatments that doctors developed by the turn of the twentieth century. Most cholera treatments are based on various types of saline solutions. In the 1950s, Indian doctors developed an inexpensive and successful treatment called **oral rehydration therapy (ORT)**. ORT is a drinkable solution containing necessary salts. Another, more costly, therapy is used for severely dehydrated patients. **Fluid replacement therapy (FRT)** requires an IV and must be given in a hospital or clinic. In the 1960s, doctors discovered that recovery is faster when the ORT or FRT contains a sugar called glucose. Glucose helps transport the salts through the membranes of the intestine and into the body, where the salts help retain fluids. Other researchers have suggested giving patients food containing starch in addition to ORT because the body converts starch into glucose.

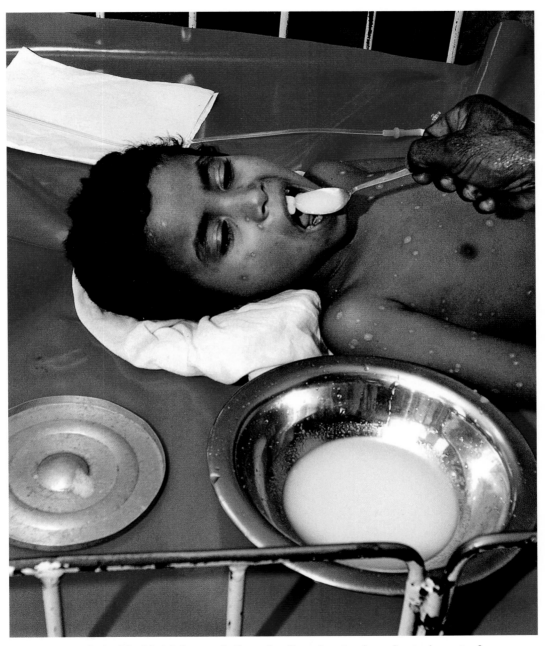

A young Bangladeshi girl drinks a solution of salt and water in order to keep to from dehydrating.

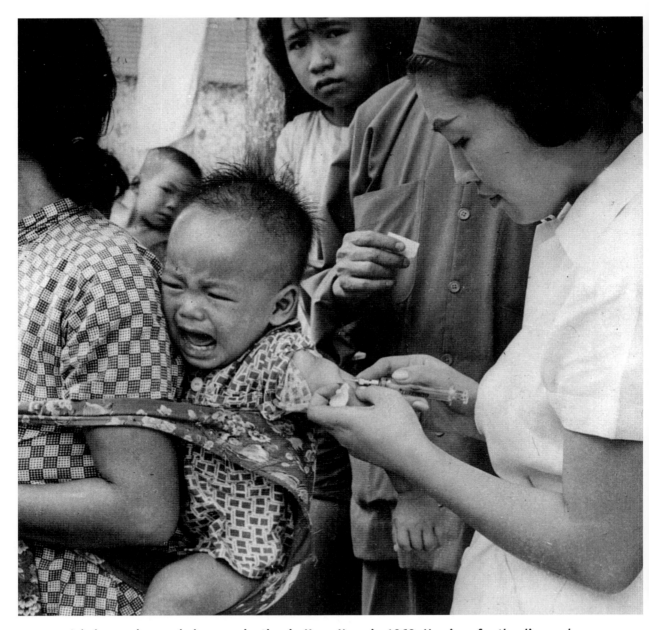

A baby receives a cholera vaccination in Hong Kong in 1963. Vaccines for the disease have been developed, but they do not last long.

Doctors are also attempting to find **vaccines** to prevent cholera. So far, many of them have proved ineffective for extensive lengths of time. Japanese researchers have experimented with using a crop-based vaccine that would encourage people's immune systems to fight several bacterial diseases, including cholera. Korean doctors have developed a vaccine that was influenced by the work of Vietnamese researchers. Now that WHO has approved this vaccine, a drug company in India plans to distribute it in cholera-prone areas.

Doctors around the world agree that cholera is relatively simple to fight compared to other contagious bacterial infections. In industrialized countries, good sanitary conditions have virtually wiped out cholera. The biggest problem for doctors and researchers is how to cure and prevent cholera in impoverished, war-torn, or disaster-stricken areas of the world.

4

LIVING WITH CHOLERA

Most people who ingest the cholera bacteria never know it. They do not become sick, or if they do have a bout of stomach upset or mild diarrhea, they might not realize that *Vibrio cholerae* is the reason. But whether or not a person becomes ill, the bacteria can live in his or her body for up to two weeks, so it is highly possible that infected bodily wastes will pollute water supplies and sicken other people. Cholera directly affects people who are in close contact with one another. Whenever a person suspects he or she has been exposed to cholera, the individual must take very careful steps to avoid spreading the disease. In addition to promoting individual responsibility for preventing the spread of cholera, governments and health organizations must also do their part by protecting water supplies, educating the public about proper hygiene, and managing waste and sewage disposal.

TREATMENT

As deadly as cholera can be, it is easy to treat. The first line of defense against the disease is to restore fluids lost through diarrhea and vomiting. This can be as simple as drinking a solution of water, sugar, and salt. Called ORS, or oral rehydration solution, this basic mixture contains sodium chloride and glucose. The mixture must be prepared properly because certain ratios of these ingredients are required, and too much salt can be dangerous. Different forms of sugar and salt can be used. WHO and UNICEF (United Nations Children's Fund) have approved several ORS solutions. Most cholera victims can be treated with ORS, but some people are severely dehydrated and require **rehydrating** with IV liquids for at least four hours.

Once their fluid levels are brought into balance, patients with cholera must continue drinking ORS for several days until their diarrhea subsides. For some people, it may be necessary to take **antibiotics** to help combat the bacterial infection. The antibiotic tetracycline usually reduces the length of time it takes for a person to recover. However, many scientists worry that cholera bacteria are growing resistant to tetracycline. There are other effective drugs, but they are more expensive and less available antibiotics. Also, the threat of the cholera

Famous People Who
Fell Victim to Cholera

....

- James Knox Polk, the eleventh U.S. president
- King Charles X of France
- Pyotr Ilyich Tchaikovsky, composer of *The Nutcracker* and the *1812 Overture*
- Georg Wilhelm Friedrich Hegel, German philosopher
- Moritz Thomsen, author and Peace Corps worker
- Relatives of the following people: Robert Frost; U.S. presidents Andrew Jackson, Millard Fillmore, and Barack Obama; Daniel Boone; Harriet Beecher Stowe; General George Custer; Mary Shelley.

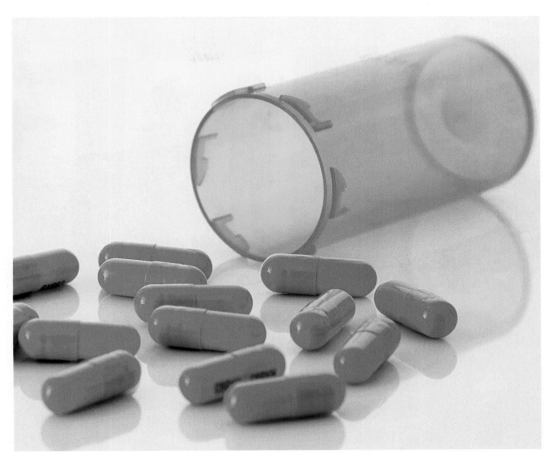

Antibiotics are an important part of a treatment plan for cholera.

bacteria mutating into a form resistant to *any* drug is frightening.

Finally, after rehydration and antibiotics, there is one more treatment step. Health care workers encourage patients to resume eating healthful foods. This gives their bodies strength to recover fully.

A young girl in Guinea stands under an advertisement for Orasel oral rehydration salts (ORS). ORS are 95% effective at saving the lives of dehydrated children.

PREVENTION

Countries with good sanitation practices have almost completely prevented cholera from occurring. But even for people who live in areas where cholera is common—and for people traveling to those areas—there are several means of preventing sickness. First and foremost is to follow good hygiene: to keep hands clean, to drink only purified or boiled water, and not to eat raw vegetables unless they have been washed in clean water or cooked to a temperature that kills bacteria. People should also avoid eating raw seafood, beans, and grains that have been cooked but allowed to sit at room temperature for a long time.

Vaccines are an effective way to prevent many diseases, and several medical research companies have created vaccines to fight cholera. But generally the vaccines are ineffective over time. Doctors also worry that people who are vaccinated become careless about hygiene or about what they eat and drink. Nearly all cholera outbreaks occur in remote and impoverished locations, and that makes it all the more difficult for medical workers to provide vaccinations for everyone in a community. Vaccines have other drawbacks as well: they are expensive, and they must be carefully stored so that they stay fresh. Scientists in Vietnam claim that a new oral vaccine will protect people who take only two doses. This vaccine is also much less expensive than other vaccines. Health organizations

In order to try and prevent a cholera outbreak, villagers in South Africa use a water monitoring kit to make sure the river water is safe to drink.

are hopeful that the vaccines will reduce the number of major cholera outbreaks.

CHOLERA IN THE WORLD TODAY

Cholera provides few health concerns for countries with good public sanitation systems, but it still mortally affects millions of people living in impoverished areas of the world. Communities most at risk are overcrowded urban areas in developing countries, where clean water and public sewage systems are in scant supply. Also highly at risk for cholera are people living in areas that suffer from the effects of war or natural disasters. Following a disaster, clean water and sewage treatment systems can break down. In many of these situations, displaced people take shelter in large refugee camps. Refugee camps are usually pulled together quickly, and they rarely have clean water supplies and waste disposal systems. Cholera can spread swiftly under these conditions.

During such disasters, local governments are overwhelmed. International aid organizations sometimes come to the rescue. They set up refugee camps, transport food and freshwater to the site, and establish makeshift medical clinics. It is a vast undertaking, and a cholera outbreak looms as a cruel threat. Refugee camp workers remind people about the importance of washing their hands after using the toilet. Children are told to avoid playing in puddles of dirty water. Clean drinking water

Cholera outbreaks still happen in developing countries because clean drinking water is not always available. Here, Iraqis fill a pan with drinking water from a burst water pipe.

Cholera Kit

· · · · · · · · · · · · · · · · ·

When cholera strikes, aid organizations rush to the afflicted site to provide preventive care and treatment. They welcome the arrival of cholera kits, which are essential supplies packaged by large organizations such as the Red Cross, WHO, World Vision, and UNICEF. A cholera kit usually contains the following items:

- large tents that can accommodate up to fifty patients at a time
- refrigerators
- portable generators
- cots
- portable toilets or latrines
- IV equipment
- rehydration solutions
- water tanks
- water purification tablets
- soap
- hand and foot baths

is often in short supply, and refugee camp workers sometimes have to battle with people to convince them to avoid dirty water and to drink only purified water. It is difficult to convince hungry, thirsty refugees to follow rules of sanitation. In addition, many people are not used to water purified with chlorine bleach, so it tastes foreign and unpleasant. Yet chlorine is the easiest, cheapest, and most effective way to kill bacteria in water.

Cholera bacteria are not likely to vanish from Earth anytime soon. However, humankind has the means to stop this disease from reaching pandemic proportions. Affordable new vaccines are being developed. Disaster relief groups are becoming more organized in getting enough medical supplies to cholera-stricken areas quickly. Governments of wealthier nations, as well as international aid organizations, are educating and supporting the governments of developing countries as they build and improve sanitation controls. And the world is keeping a watchful eye on cholera. Using satellite images, maps, and other data, scientists can predict outbreaks before they become widespread. With this helpful information, aid workers can arrive at the scene and prevent an epidemic from taking hold. Although the African nation of Zimbabwe is currently suffering an epidemic, recently affected countries such as Rwanda and Democratic Republic of the Congo (DRC) have moved forward in developing new sanitation projects. DRC

UNICEF sent a tank of freshwater to Zimbabwe in December 2008 during a cholera outbreak that had killed nearly six hundred people.

officials hope that by the year 2012 they will have pipes to deliver clean water to communities so that the people can stop using surface water, water from unfiltered wells, and water taken directly from rivers and lakes. India, Vietnam, Malaysia, and other cholera-prone areas are also working on ways to protect their citizens. Modern technology and communication have connected the nations of the world more closely. And it will take the unified effort of all nations to manage cholera outbreaks and to prevent them from destroying lives.

GLOSSARY

antibiotics—Medications that fight bacterial infections.

bacterium—A microscopic organism composed of a single cell (*plural* bacteria).

contamination—The presence of harmful microorganisms in food or water.

copepods—Tiny sea creatures that carry cholera bacteria.

cholera toxin (CTX)—A poisonous, disease-causing substance created by cholera bacteria.

dehydration—A lack of necessary bodily fluids.

diarrhea—Frequent or unusually watery bowel movements.

electrolytes—Salts in blood, tissue, fluids, and cells (such as sodium, potassium, and chlorine) that regulate the fluid levels of the body.

endemic—Existing in a certain region.

epidemic—A fast-moving outbreak of a disease that infects many people at the same time.

epidemiology—The science of studying patterns and occurrences of diseases among groups of people.

feces—Solid waste excreted from the body.

fluid replacement therapy (FRT)—A treatment in which a solution of salts and sugar is injected into a person's veins to restore his or her fluid levels.

hypoglycemia—A condition that occurs when a person's blood sugar level drops too low.

hypovolemic shock—A condition caused by a sudden drop in blood flow through the body.

intravenous (IV)—Delivered directly into a vein through a hollow needle.

miasma—"Bad air" that was supposed to transmit diseases in the nineteenth century.

microorganisms—Microscopic organisms, including bacteria, viruses, fungi, plants, parasites, and animals.

oral rehydration therapy (ORT)—A treatment in which a person drinks a solution of water, glucose, and salts to restore his or her body fluids.

outbreaks—Sudden, unexpected occurrences of a disease in two or more people who have ingested the same food or drink.

rehydrating—Restoring lost water to the body tissues and fluids.

sanitary—Clean; free of germs.

sewage—Liquid and solid waste from the human body.

strain—Related groups that have slightly different characteristics.

symptoms—The signs of an illness.

vaccines—Substances made from an infectious organism that causes an immune response that prevents disease.

Vibrio cholerae—The bacterium that causes cholera.

water purification—A process that filters out bacteria and other harmful substances from the water supply.

FIND OUT MORE

Organizations

International Federation of Red Cross and Red Crescent Societies

P.O. Box 372
CH-1211 Geneva 19
Switzerland
Telephone: +41 22 730 42 22

UNICEF House

3 United Nations Plaza
44th Street
New York, NY 10016
Telephone: 212-326-7000

World Health Organization

Avenue Appia 20
1211 Geneva 27
Switzerland
Telephone: + 41 22 791 21 11

Books

Coleman, William. *Cholera*. New York: Chelsea House, 2008.

Peters, Stephanie True. *Cholera: Curse of the Nineteenth Century*. New York: Benchmark Books, 2004.

Walker, Richard. *Epidemics and Plagues*. New York: Kingfisher, 2007.

Websites

Centers for Disease Control and Prevention: www.cdc.gov/nczved/dfbmd/disease_listing/cholera_gi.html

Doctors Without Borders: http://doctorswithoutborders.org/news/issue.cfm?id=2390

Travelers' Precautions: http://kidshealth.org/teen/medications/travelers_diarrhea_and_cholera_vaccine.html

World Health Organization Cholera Factsheet: www.who.int/mediacentre/factsheets/fs107/en/index.htm

World Vision Fact Sheet www.worldvision.org/content.nsf/about/emergency-presskit-zimbabwe-cholera-faq

INDEX

ABOUT THE AUTHOR

Ruth Bjorklund lives on Bainbridge Island, a ferry ride away from Seattle, Washington, with her husband, two children, and five pets. She has written several books about health issues.